Program Notes

...natic and brilliantly colored score for the motion picture "LAWRENCE OF ARABIA" introduced a new young French composer, Maurice Jarre, to American audiences. Working with the usual symphonic instrumentation plus additional percussion and two new electronic instruments at that time: the onde martinote and the cithare, he had created a musical setting of the utmost power and beauty, setting off the exotic story of T. E. Lawrence perfectly, and complementing the visual picture with a tonal one of tremendous impact.

This arrangement for symphonic band is built upon two of the three main themes: the Arabian motif, with its blazing color and almost-barbaric effects; and the Lawrence theme, a haunting, poignant melody that reflects both his love of the desert and his internal, psychological conflicts. The music opens with the Arabian motif, developed at length from the timpani figure in the woodwinds, saxophones and a single cornet, and then sweeps up into the full band, to be played as broadly and lyrically as possible. To complete the musical form, the Arabian theme returns, and after a brief reminder of the Lawrence theme combined with it, brings the music to a dramatic conclusion.

Notes to the Conductor

The conductor is urged to consider the following points carefully in preparing this music for performance:

1. The percussion is as important as the rest of the band, especially in the opening section; and must always play cleanly and with a clear sound that will "ring" clearly through the musical texture at every point ... without, of course, completely over-powering it.

2. The tempo at the beginning and up to measure [27] as well as at the return to Tempo I° later on, should be played only as fast as the timpani can play its complex figures clearly and cleanly. The timpani should play with hard and medium-hard <u>felt</u> sticks only.

3. The suspended cymbal should be as large as possible, and struck only with a medium-hard felt mallet. The pair of cymbals, on the other hand, should be as small as possible, as to produce a light "shimmering" sound, to approximate the true Arabian instruments.

4. The tom-toms should be as far apart in pitch as possible; the idea being to make them sound like a small pair of timpani. Hard felt sticks should be used throughout.

5. A metal beater should always be used on the triangle.

6. The tempo, beginning at measure [27] should not be too slow; the music here should give a broad effect, but never drag. Watch the dynamics, phrase and expression marks carefully in order to obtain the most lyrical effect possible.

7. The B-flat cornet parts should be played on actual cornets, and the trumpet parts played on trumpets for maximum color differentiation in the upper brass.

8. The timpani "interjections" from measure [27] through the return to Tempo I° should always be heard clearly, as a sort of "reminder-motive" of the Arabian theme throughout this section.

Careful attention to detail will result in a brilliant, rousing performance of this exciting music.

ALFRED REED

Lawrence of Arabia
for Concert Band
by
Maurice Jarre
Arranged by Alfred Reed
Edited by R. Mark Rogers

INSTRUMENTATION

1-FULL SCORE	2-1st TRUMPETS
1-PICCOLO	2-2nd TRUMPETS
3-1st FLUTES	2-3rd TRUMPETS
3-2nd FLUTES	1-1st CORNET
1-1st OBOE	1-2nd CORNET
1-2nd OBOE	1-1st HORN in F
1-CLARINET in E-flat	1-2nd HORN in F
4-1st CLARINETS	1-3rd HORN in F
4-2nd CLARINETS	1-4th HORN in F
4-3rd CLARINETS	2-1st TROMBONES
1-ALTO CLARINET	2-2nd TROMBONES
2-BASS CLARINETS	2-3rd TROMBONES
1-CONTRA ALTO or	3-EUPHONIUMS (T.C./ B.C.)
CONTRA BASS CLARINET	4-TUBAS
1-1st BASSOONS	1-STRING BASS
1-2nd BASSOONS	1-TIMPANI (3 DRUMS)
2-1st ALTO SAXOPHONES	4-PERCUSSION
2-2nd ALTO SAXOPHONES	*Suspended Cym., Triangle, Tom-*
2-TENOR SAXOPHONES	*Toms, Bass Dr., Crash Cym.*
1-BARITONE SAXOPHONE	2-MALLET PERCUSSION
	Bells, Vibraphone

Grade 4
Duration:
  Approx. 4 Minutes

Theme from "Lawrence of Arabia" from LAWRENCE OF ARABIA by Maurice Jarre
Copyright © 1962 Screen Gems-EMI Music Inc. Copyright renewed.
This arrangement Copyright © 2016 Screen Gems-EMI Music Ind.
All Rights Administered by Sony/ATV Music Publishing LLC, 424 Church Street, Suite 1200, Nashville, TN 37219
International copyright secured. All Rights Reserved. Reprinted by Permission of Hal Leonard Corporation.

Theme from
LAWRENCE OF ARABIA

Full Score
S947

MAURICE JARRE
arranged by ALFRED REED
edited by R. Mark Rogers

S947: Lawrence of Arabia

S947: Lawrence of Arabia

poco allarg. **Tempo I - Fast, driving**

S947: Lawrence of Arabia

S947: Lawrence of Arabia

S947: Lawrence of Arabia

S947: Lawrence of Arabia

Alfred Reed

Alfred Reed (January 25, 1921, - September 17, 2005) was a prolific and frequently performed composer, with more than two hundred published works for concert band, wind ensemble, orchestra, chorus, and chamber ensemble to his name. He also traveled extensively as a guest conductor, performing in North America, Latin America, Europe and Asia.

Reed was born in New York and began his formal music training at the age of ten. During World War II, he served in the 529th Army Air Force Band. Following his military service, he attended the Juilliard School of Music, studying under Vittorio Giannini, after which he was staff composer and arranger first for NBC, then for ABC. In 1953, he became the conductor of the Baylor Symphony Orchestra at Baylor University, where he received his B.M. in 1955 and his M.M. in 1956. His master's thesis, *Rhapsody for Viola and Orchestra*, was awarded the Luria Prize in 1959. He was a member of the Beta Tau Chapter of Phi Mu Alpha Sinfonia, the national fraternity for men in music.

From 1955 to 1966, he was the executive editor of Hansen Publications, a music publisher. He was professor of music at the University of Miami where he worked with composer Clifton Williams from 1966 until his death in 1976. Williams' office was across the hall from Reed's office in the UM School of Music, and Reed was chairman of the department of Music Media and Industry and director of the Music Industry Program at the time of his retirement. He established the very first college-level music business curriculum at the University of Miami in 1966, which led other colleges and universities to follow suit. At the time of his death, he had composition commissions that would have taken him to the age of 115. Many of Reed's wind band compositions have been released as CD recordings by the Tokyo Kosei Wind Orchestra.

R. Mark Rogers

R. Mark Rogers has degrees from Texas Tech University and the University of Texas. As Director of Publications for Southern Music Company from 1993 through 2012, he authored editions of the music of Percy Grainger and John Philip Sousa that have entered band repertory worldwide. He is also widely published as an arranger and transcriber, with performances by all five of the Washington, DC service bands. Dr. Rogers is the conductor of the Heart of Texas Concert Band and serves on the adjunct faculty of San Antonio College, Texas Lutheran University and Trinity University, and prior to coming to San Antonio was on the faculty of the University of South Alabama and a staff member with the University of Texas Longhorn Band. A bassoonist, he performs with the orchestras of Corpus Christi, Victoria, Laredo, San Antonio and Austin, as well as the Mid-Texas Symphony. He is active in church music and occasionally appears in music theater, including numerous roles in the operettas of Gilbert and Sullivan. Sudie, his wife of forty years, his children and their spouses (and grandchild), are the joy of his later years.

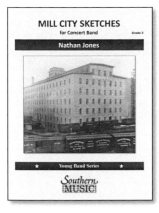

NATHAN JONES - MILL CITY SKETCHES

This exciting tone poem was inspired by American entrepreneurs of the Industrial Revolution, portraying the dynamic early flour industry in Minneapolis and the dramatic historical events surrounding explosion of the Washburn A Mill. This rhapsodic work features soaring melodic lines, driving rhythms, and interesting parts for each instrument. The scoring is pleasantly open and transparent while maintaining plentiful doublings to ensure balance and secure playing across sections of the band.
(Grade 3) Dur: 5:00
HL00147329 – S941CB Score/Parts..$65.00
HL00147330 – S941FS Full Score.......$9.95

ERIC EWAZEN - TATTOO

Tattoo is the stirring finale of *Legacy*, commissioned for the bicentennial celebration of West Point. The opening theme "Tattoo" is based on the bugle call which signals a return to quarters at day's end. The score includes antiphonal effects with optional offstage bugles and field drum, creating an authentic "military" sound. The old West Point song "Benny Havens" leads into the reemerging "Tattoo" theme, now answered by other bugle calls, bringing the work to a rousing conclusion.
(Grade 4) Dur: 6:00
HL00144838 – S939CB Score/Parts..$99.00
HL00144839 – S939FS Full Score.....$20.00

BERNHARD HEIDEN - DIVERSION FOR ALTO SAXOPHONE AND BAND

Edited by R. Mark Rogers
Composed while Bernhard Heiden served as Assistant Bandmaster for the 445th US Army band during World War II, this first-ever print edition has been carefully edited and adapted with modern instrumentation. The influence of the composer's mentor, Paul Hindemith is evident in the tonal yet nondiatonic harmonies, paired with Heiden's own light and tuneful melodic writing.
(Grade 4) Dur: 7:00
HL00137320 – S938CB Score/Parts..$75.00
HL00137321 – S938FS Full Score.....$15.00

ERIC EWAZEN - A HYMN FOR THE LOST AND THE LIVING

Arranged for Trombone Choir
by Chris Sharpe
This gorgeous setting is dedicated to Vern and Jan Kagarice and was premiered by University of North Texas Trombone Choir. The work portrays the days in the aftermath of September 11, 2001 of supreme sadness and surprising resilience as the country mourned a great loss while coming together for help, comfort, and strength.
(Grade 5) Dur: 9:00
HL00142908 – SU788 Score/Parts $44.95
HL00146041 – SU788FS Full Score ..$14.95

JAMES BARNES - SYMPHONIC REQUIEM (SEVENTH SYMPHONY)

Commissioned for the United States Army Band to commemorate the 150th Anniversary of the American Civil War, the work combines two massive structures into one: a requiem and a symphony. It portrays the heartbreak of three of the most dramatic battles of the war, concluded by an apotheosis, a hymn of respect and praise for the 668,000 soldiers, Confederate and Federal alike, who gave their lives during this monumental conflict.
(Grade 5) Dur: 28:00
HL00147324 – S940CB Score/Parts$225.00
HL00147325 – S940FS Full Score $38.95

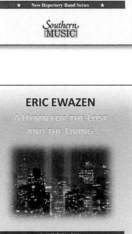

THE NEW YORK WOODWIND QUINTET LIBRARY SERIES

Considered by many as the greatest woodwind quintet in the world, this all-star ensemble has transcribed many classic masterpieces from other genres over their 70-year history. Southern Music is proud to present the NYWQ Library Series which makes this repertoire available to all woodwind quintets for the first time ever.
DVORAK "AMERICAN" STR. QUARTET NO. 12
HL00124645 – SU781 ....$65.00
MOZART STR. QUARTET NO. 14, "SPRING"
HL00124646 – SU782 ....$65.00
MOZART FANTASY, KV 594
HL00142906 – SU786 ....$24.95
MOZART FANTASY, KV 608
HL00142907 – SU787 ....$24.95